THE L BETWEEN US

A SHORT STORY

PRAISE FOR THE DRINKS BETWEEN US

"A raw tale of alcoholism and neglect that hits hard yet instills hope. A superb story!"
— Terry Lander, Author of *Banned* and *Red Light London*

"A meditation on grief and trauma from one generation to the next, *The Drinks Between Us* is a swift read that explores what creates broken people, addiction, and the lows between the highs."
— Keanu Joaquin Del Toro, Author of *The Eve Of Our Generation*

"A story about a father and son that teaches empathy and expertly demonstrates the fickle nature of memory and perspective. A great story for anyone interested in reading about relationships between parents and their children, fathers and sons, grief, and moving on.
— Marlene Ridgway, Author of *Where Is She?*

"This short story was fantastic. My heart felt every ounce of emotion between ALL of the characters. I've read it three times already and my heart still gets invested in it all. *The Drinks Between Us* has helped me move forward with my own relationship with my father."
— Megan Maher (starred review)

"*The Drinks Between Us* is a moving story of a family working through grief in different ways. It's an eye-opening look into how children view their parents in times of extreme hardships. Vince does an excellent job at conveying the heartbreaks and triumphs of life in a broken family."
— Cassie Van Stone (starred review)

*Disclaimer: Reviews have been edited for clarity and length

Cover Art Copyright © 2022 by Indie Earth Publishing
Section Illustration Copyright © 2022 by X.Style Studio

Edited by Flor Ana Mireles

1st Edition | 01
Paperback ISBN: 978-1-7379393-8-2

First Published July 2022

For inquiries and bulk orders, please email:
indieearthpublishinghouse@gmail.com

Indie Earth Publishing Inc.
| Miami, FL |

INDIE EARTH
PUBLISHING

"As you were, I was. As I am, you will be."

Hunter S. Thompson

To Mom, Dad, Megan, Anthony, and Larry

*And a special dedication to every father,
for we truly do not know how much they bare for us.*

Warning: This book discusses topics of alchol and drug use as well as physical and emotional abuse.

PROLOGUE

A father's love is unconditional, but we reap what he sows.
We all have a picture in our heads of what a perfect father should
look and act like. Strong and handsome, our personal hero, a man
that can do no wrong. But, sometimes, the reality is that our fathers
are not the men we build them up to be in our minds.

THE MAIN STREET BAR
South Jersey, NJ | Spring 2018

"**D**id your father ever play catch with you?"

Like many insightful conversations about John's father, one early afternoon, this one started at the bar. John had walked in a few moments before, already in a mood. He was on his second beer when a man sitting a few stools away from him decided to strike up a conversation after seeing a car commercial about a father and son playing catch.

The commercial ended with one of those cheesy taglines.

"Don't miss out on those memories!"

John looked over at the guy who was smiling and assumed he must have kids or admired his father.

"The only catch I played was when my father would throw empty beer bottles at me and yell, 'Go get me another one...' The cans were so much better than the bottles," John replied.

The man looked stunned, almost sorry he'd asked.

"I'm sure your father wasn't always horrible to you," he said.

"Not always. Sometimes, he would take me to baseball games and teach me the game."

The man smiled, feeling relieved.

"See, I knew it couldn't be all that bad!" he said.

John's face turned red as he turned to the man and yelled,

"Yeah, until he got drunk at the game and I'd have to hail us a cab home because he was too drunk to drive."

"Whoa, sorry, buddy... Sounds like your dad had some problems. Did he ever try quitting?"

John looked back at the man, and, with a stone-cold face, replied, "My father said, 'Don't be a quitter, son... There are already too many of those in this world.'"

"Your father sounds like a wise man!" the man said, lightening the air.

"My father was an asshole and a drunk. That's just something he would say so that he wouldn't feel bad about getting wasted all day. The fact was my father couldn't quit even if he tried!" John replied.

Suddenly, the man stood up, finished his beer, paid his tab, and left.

John sat there for a few minutes looking around, feeling puzzled about what just happened. He sat there thinking about what had set him off.

It's not like he knows my father... Why would he get so mad? John thought. *Maybe he was mad at how much contempt I have for my father? How damaged he makes me feel because of him, or maybe he has romanticized the idea of fathers, as so many other people do. A father is supposed to be strong and wise, all-knowing, and confident. Not weak and incompetent, lost and timid. Was his father one of these weak men? Maybe that's why he left. I must have shattered his idea of fathers... That's it! All this time he believed fathers were infallible until he met me and now he realized his father is just like everyone else's, just a man.*

John sat there staring at the condensation on the side of his beer.

Was it all his fault? he asked himself. *Did my father fuck everything up for me, or have I just used him as an excuse to get fucked up all these years?*

John continued staring as another bead of water went dripping down the glass. He picked up the bottle, finished what was left, and placed it back on the bar. As John pushed it towards the bartender, he could see he wasn't pleased.

"Do me a favor, turn it down a notch," the bartender said, putting another beer in front of John.

"What for?" John said, looking around, "There are two people in here and neither of them are listening."

The two regulars John referred to had been sitting in one of the booths behind him, playing chess. The small rectangular bar had a row of booths along the wall opposite the counter, and a jukebox right next to the hallway entrance to the bathroom.

The bartender—his nametag showcasing a barely visible *Ben*—stood there with an apathetic look on his face watching the TV.

"That's why I stop watching the news, too many people, with too many problems. What the fuck do I care about other people's problems for?" John said, taking another swig of beer.

"And why should we care about *your* problems?" Ben said, annoyed.

He took a deep breath, trying to keep his patience.

"Listen, sometimes life's going to shit on you. It's what you do after it that makes you who you are. Do you just sit there smelling like shit for the rest of your life, or do you wash up, change your clothes, and try to feel like a new man again?"

"Huh?" John said, looking confused.

"Okay, enough with the psychobabble. Either you sit here, shut the fuck up, and drink in peace or find somewhere else to cry in your drink. Deal?" said the bartender as he pointed toward the door.

"...Deal," John mumbled under his breath as he sat there staring at the counter like a dog with his tail between his legs.

The bartender stood there for a few seconds, watching the TV as John contemplated his life.

Maybe he's right, John thought. *Maybe I've been wallowing in self-pity for too long and need to wash the funk off me... But was it funk, or was it a part of me, something that I couldn't just wash away? Lord knows I would have if I could. Maybe he's wrong. Maybe he's just trying to say that bad things happen to good people, and I shouldn't let that affect me... Well, this wasn't just one bad thing. There were a multitude of bad things over a long period of time... What do you call that then?* John pondered. *A shitty life, I guess.*

"So, what's it going to be?" the bartender asked, "Are you done with your shit or am I going to have to make you leave?"

John looked up, annoyed, and replied, "I'm quiet, ain't I? How about you stop standing there and do your job. Go grab me another beer!"

John slammed the beer down, almost breaking the bottle on the edge of the bar.

"No one asked you to be my therapist. Why don't you keep your fat nose out of my business!" John said, pointing the bottle's mouth to the bartender.

The bartender turned around, looking enraged, and snapped back.

"Watch it, you little shit! Don't make me throw your ass out of here! I don't have time for you. Trust me! I've taken shits that were bigger than you, you hear me!"

Anger filled up John's body, boiling up like a pot of water on a fiery stove. John stood up and motioned like he was about to leave, but his legs were so wobbly from sitting so long that he quickly sat back down.

"Listen, I'm done talking… Can I just have a glass of water? I promise I'll behave."

"Fine," the bartender mumbled as he walked to the other side of the bar to grab ice for the glass and poured water from a pitcher.

"Here, you ungrateful little shit," he said, as he placed the glass down in front of him, splashing some of the water onto the counter.

"Who pissed in your cheerios?" John said under his breath as he watched the bartender walk to the other end of the bar, looking for anything else to do besides talk to him.

The door opened and the sunlight shone in, cascading into the bar like a waterfall, only showing part of the face of the lonely patron as he walked in. The door shut behind him, blackening the dimly lit bar again. The three o'clock news had begun, and the theme song could be heard as the door opened. The two men in the booth took a break from their chess game to pick out songs on the jukebox, resulting in an argument over which classic rock song was the best.

"Don't you make this guy run off, he's been coming here for years," Ben said as he walked past John.

"Fuck you," John whispered to himself as he played with the coaster.

"Welcome back. What can I get for you, Mike?" Ben said to the man who had just walked in.

The man paused for a second before answering as he took a seat at the corner of the bar counter nearest the wooden door.

"I'll have a whiskey and a beer."

John thought he recognized the voice, although he couldn't

make out the man's face.

"And give that guy a beer. No sense sitting in a bar without having a drink in your hand," Mike said, eying the water in front of John.

The bartender looked peeved as he placed a shot of whiskey in front of Mike and proceeded to pop two fresh beers open. He walked down to where John was sitting, and placed the beer in front of him.

"Don't fuck this up," the bartender whispered as John twirled his coaster like a spinning top.

"Just do your job and shut up!" John answered.

Not even looking up as he took his beer, the bartender walked away.

"What's his problem?" Mike asked.

"Oh, he just has daddy issues. Don't mind him, and for damn sure, don't start a conversation with him," the bartender replied with a stern voice.

"Don't we all!" said the man as he took the shot of whiskey and pounded the glass down on the counter.

"Life's too short, kid!" Mike shouted at John.

"What'd you say?" he replied.

"Life's too short to worry about the past! Everyone's got shitty dads, even me!"

John chuckled to himself.

"Yeah, I bet," he said.

In the background, the two men had finished picking songs and returned to their booth, commencing another silent game of chess.

"What did he ever do to you to make you hate him so much?" Mike said as he sipped his beer.

"Didn't I tell you not to start with him?" Ben said, wiping

down the countertop.

"I got this," he whispered, "I know a thing or two about being a father."

The bartender stepped back, a look of contempt on his face.

"So, like I said, what did this guy ever do to you to make you hate him so much?" Mike reiterated.

John sat there for a minute, confused as to who this guy thought he was.

"My father was an asshole drunk who did nothing but work all day and drink all night. And when he wasn't drinking, he was treating us like shit," John said, his face getting redder by the minute.

"Where was your mom during all this?" Mike asked, taking another sip of his beer.

"Up in heaven. Cancer killed her when I was just a kid."

John's face became red as he lowered his head. The room fell silent for a minute, only music from the jukebox and the TV filling the bar. The two men had stopped their game and started paying attention for a moment.

"Can I get another one?" John said as he finished his beer.

"Yeah, this one is on me, kid," Ben said as he put down another drink in front of John.

It wasn't the first time Ben had men coming into the bar with their losses. The man across the bar sighed as he pushed his empty beer bottle to the edge of the bar.

Ben began walking over to pick up the bottle as Mike said, "Did you ever think that maybe your dad was going through something? Maybe he was having trouble raising kids and grieving for his dead wife all at the same time. Did you ever think about that?"

"Listen, man, I don't know who you are, but you didn't live in that house with him. You don't know how it was," John shouted across the room, his hands shaking as he reached for his beer.

"Aww, I'm sure you were a real treat, too! Hit me with another drink, Ben!" Mike said.

Ben stood there quietly for a moment before moving.

"I think both of you guys need to cool it before you make me close up for the day. I'm tired of this shit today, man!" he said.

Mike couldn't help but feel he recognized the kid across the bar from somewhere. Perhaps, the grown-up child of an old friend.

"Where are you from, kid?" Mike asked as he pulled his fresh shot glass closer to him, trying not to spill the liquor that was poured to the top.

"Just around the corner. What's it to you?" John said in his most sarcastic tone.

"Just asking is all... You little shit... Haven't you heard of bar conversations?" Mike said, shaking his head.

John got up abruptly and walked outside. He lit a cigarette and began pacing back and forth while exhaling aggressively.

Who the fuck does this guy think he is? Fuck him. He doesn't know me or what I've been through.

He finished his cigarette and walked back inside. When he sat down, he took a second to think about the last time he had been to his father's house.

The last time John saw his father, he was walking out of the front door. He was only a young man, and his father was screaming, "If that door opens and you walk out, don't think it's going to open for you again!"

John had heard those kinds of statements all too often. His father taunted him every night after he'd been drinking for most of the afternoon.

"You know why you're so weak, it's because you're a sissy. Don't worry, son, you'll never amount to anything anyways. Who could ever love a little piece of shit like you?"

He would continue to berate John until he would turn away to leave, broken and confused. He couldn't understand what made his father so mad every time they were together.

1058 SERRILL AVENUE
South Jersey, NJ | Summer 1973

John's father, Jack, had a tough life. He lived most of his childhood with his grandparents due to his parents splitting up when he was in grade school and, for that reason, he was very quiet when it came to his emotions. That first night when he moved into their place, he cried about missing his mother, which resulted in his grandmother smacking him across his mouth.

Jack began to cry more loudly until she said, "Shut that shit up. No one's coming for you, so stop all that crying!"

Jack stood there quietly, wiping the tears from his eyes. His lip quivered from fear and sadness. He knew his grandmother didn't like to repeat herself. So, he turned to walk away before she could smack him again for not listening.

That was the last day that Jack cried.

He grew up to become a handsome young man, tall and athletic, towering well over six feet. While in high school, he played football. He was never the captain of the team, but he played every game, all the way up to the winning championship his senior year. After graduation, Jack knew he wasn't destined for college, not to mention his grandparents' savings didn't amount to much. Since he couldn't afford it either, Jack was left with only a few options: join the military or find a job. He knew he didn't want to fight, so he had to think about what he was good at. He'd always had a fascination for cars, so he woke up, walked down to the bank, and asked for a small business loan to open his mechanic shop.

He wore a buzzed cut most days, but when his hair would grow out, it was a dark brown. He was a hard worker and people in the town trusted him with their cars. He always made sure to take his time to explain exactly what was going on with them. He wanted to make sure they knew they were safe to drive their families around town, and if they couldn't afford to pay that day, he would set up a payment plan for them so they could get back to work.

It was a few months into the third year of the shop when Jack met Margaret. She was so sweet and kind, and she smelled of summer rain. Her eyes were the color of honey, golden and pure. Her hair was auburn, the color of autumn and changing leaves. When they saw each other for the first time, they locked eyes. Jack was stunned by how gorgeous she was.

She had called for a tow and needed to have her car dropped off at the shop. She was so frustrated about being late and worried about her students, but Jack was a gentleman and took his time to explain how long it would take for her car to get done. In the meantime, he offered to drop her off at the school so she wouldn't be any later than she already was.

A few weeks later, they met again while waiting in line for coffee. Jack had finished his order and began walking toward the other end of the counter when he heard a familiar voice. It was Margaret. As she walked toward him, she looked up and smiled.

"Hi, Jack, right?" Margaret said.

"Yes. Hey, how are you doing?" he asked.

"Good, thank you again for your help!"

"Of course, no problem," he replied, smiling as he grabbed his coffee to go. "I have to run, but I was wondering if you would like to go out sometime?"

Her face warmed up as she smiled and said, "Sure, you still have my number, right?"

MR. SCOOPS
South Jersey, NJ | Summer 1993

On the first date, Jack was clumsy and nervous, but Margaret knew he was trying his hardest. They went out to dinner and got to know each other for a while. After dinner, they walked down the main street to the ice cream shop. He got two scoops and she got one. They sat outside on the bench in front of the shop and talked some more. She laughed at his corny jokes and he was enamored by her wit and smile. They finished their ice cream and he walked her to her car. They both stopped for a moment, saying good night. Then, Jack kissed her. She kissed him back, and they both stared at each other for a moment before saying good night again.

What a dork, but he has caring eyes and an attractive smile, she thought.

Jack walked away thinking, *I'm surprised I didn't blow it,* with a smirk.

They went on a few more dates, Jack always trying his best to impress her and Margaret enjoying every minute of it. By the end of the year, Jack had worked up the courage to ask her to marry him. That night, they had dinner at the same restaurant they had gone to on their first date, walked down the same block, and had ice cream at the same shop. Jack and Margaret walked toward the same bench to eat their ice cream, but before she could sit down,

Jack was on one knee. In his hand was a black box with a ring in it, Margaret was so surprised that she dropped her ice cream.

I can't believe this is happening, Margaret thought.

"I know we've only known each other for a little while, but I can't see myself with anyone else… Will you marry me?" Jack asked nervously.

"Yes!" Margaret replied.

Jack's hand trembled as he put the ring on Margaret's finger.

Whoa, thank god she said yes, he thought, his heart pounding.

They had a small church wedding with some of her family and a few of his friends from the neighborhood. After the wedding, they moved into a suburban townhome. They lived a modest life, nothing too fancy, but they made it their own. Their house was just around the corner from his shop and made it easy for Jack to walk to work sometimes so Margaret could use the car to get to school on time.

She brought joy to children each morning as she began her class. Her cheerful voice could be heard in the hallways as she welcomed the children.

"Good morning, children!" her voice would sing out, as lovely as an angel.

"Good morning, Mrs. Margaret!" they would all sing back in unison.

Margaret taught first grade because she believed that kids at this age had limitless potential, and with the right love and attention, that anything was possible. Margaret had an unimaginable amount of love for children. She was a big believer in cosmic change and wanted her life to be full of purpose. This drove her to get up every day and it's what made her such a good teacher. She loved and hoped for her students as if they were her children.

It wasn't long before Jack and Margaret had children of their own. It was 1995 when Jack and Margaret brought home their first child, an adorable baby boy.

"Look how precious he looks, Jack! He's absolutely perfect," Margaret whispered.

She smiled as she handed the newborn over to his father. Jack held his son, cradling his head in his hand, John's little body, laying across Jack's strong arm. Jack's brain became flooded with so many thoughts and emotions.

He must be intelligent, brave, and loyal... There's no option, he must succeed at everything. He must achieve everything I couldn't, and be the very best out of all of us.

"Yes, he is perfect," Jack whispered.

155 WELLINGTON AVENUE
South Jersey, NJ | Autumn 1995

The ollowing year, Margaret and Jack introduced John to his baby sister Mary. The couple was overjoyed to have another child in the home. She looked like an angel, swaddled tightly in her blanket. The glowing parents stood over their sleeping child unable to look away, in awe of her magnificence.

Immediately, Jack expected John to protect Mary. It was his duty to be her shadow, to watch over her at all times when they weren't around. This pressure and expectation only increased as John grew older.

Two young children were difficult to manage, but Margaret was the ultimate mom—graceful, smart, funny, and she always had time for her children. At home, after a long day of work, she would cook a wholesome dinner for her family, get the kids washed up and ready for bed, and always have time to read them a bedtime story.

Margaret also remembered to be a caring wife, making sure she saved a little bit of energy for Jack. They had only been married a few years and didn't want the romance to die. A simple man, Jack was easy to satisfy, and she knew just what to do to make him happy. At night, when the children were asleep, they would make love and Jack would whisper in her ear, telling her how sexy she was and how incredible she made him feel. Afterward, he would hold her in his arms and think about how lucky he was.

Years passed and the children were a bit older. John was 10 and his sister, Mary trailed behind him by a year. They were close and John felt a responsibility to look after his baby sister. They were decent children, for the most part—Mary more than John. John had a problem with listening to what he was told. He, for whatever reason, felt like the rules didn't apply to him anymore, and had always been the type to question authority. He would take any chance he got to test the limits and do the complete opposite of what he was told.

That same year, Margaret started complaining of headaches. She had suffered from migraines all her life, but it never stopped her from putting a smile on her face and bringing joy to her classroom. But it became clear that her headaches were not going away.

"I think you need to go see a doctor… It's not getting better," Jack said as he put a glass of water and the bottle of aspirin down next to Margaret.

"Why? They're just going to say the same thing," Margaret replied.

"Fine, I'll make an appointment for you later this week," Jack said as Margaret put two pills in her hand and took a sip of water.

The news was a crushing blow as Jack stood there frozen, quietly repeating "No" to himself over and over as Margaret sat listening to the doctor explaining the next steps to her treatment.

The whole time, she was thinking about her children. *What about my beautiful Mary? What about my sweet Johnny?*

Margaret spent her last days in the hospital strapped to a machine with her family by her side, but, at home, Jack would stay up at night drinking and asking God why he was punishing him.

The more he would drink, the more he would curse and spit as he yelled.

The day Margaret died it was a cold and rainy September morning. It had rained for two days before and Jack had stayed at the hospital the entire time.

Minutes before she passed, Jack looked into his beautiful wife's eyes for the last time.

"I'm still the luckiest man alive," he whispered.

Jack was distraught, stricken with grief. Machines were still beeping as Jack walked straight out of the room. Overcome with emotion, he kept pacing up and down the empty hallway until he sat down in a chair in the waiting area, burying his face into his palms. The small night nurse in purple scrubs finishing up her rounds noticed Jack sitting by himself still not moving.

"Jack, I'm really sorry for your loss. I just want you to know the hospital has a grief counseling group that meets weekly if you ever want to talk to someone. Here's the director's card. Just give him a call if you want to join."

Jack was not processing what the nurse was saying. She handed him the card, which he took and stared at for a few minutes before putting it in his wallet.

Visiting Margaret every day for the past few months, Jack had become quite familiar with the area and knew there was a bar two blocks away. Without even noticing, Jack was in front of the heavy wooden door. He pushed it open and watched as the light fell into the dark bar as he walked in. He sat down, put his elbows on the counter, placed his face in his palms, and let out a deep sigh. Jack had lost everything.

"A shot of whiskey and a beer please... Make it a double, please, if you don't mind," Jack said, his face still resting in his hands.

This wasn't the first time the bartender had seen Jack this way and thought it best not to press him. He just stood quietly at the other end of the bar waiting for Jack to finish his drink before starting a conversation with him. He looked especially stressed and the bartender had a knack for reading depressed men. Finally, he had to say something.

"What's going on, Jack? You're looking extra shitty today, bud," the bartender said as he refreshed his drink.

"Not today, Ben… Margaret died this morning," Jack said as he threw back the shot and slammed the glass back on the counter.

"Jesus fucking Christ, Jack, I'm so sorry," Ben said as he walked backward, stunned and embarrassed.

"Don't be sorry, Ben. There's nothing you or I could do about it… Nothing the doctors could do either, so, you know what, Ben, I don't need your pity. Just stand there and keep pouring," Jack said, his eyes fixed on Ben.

Jack was finished. He wasn't the best father, but he cared for his children in the best way he could. When Margaret passed, something in him changed. The fire in his heart went out, and he lost the passion in his eyes. The way he looked at his children changed. Now, they were a burden, lives that needed to be taken care of, no longer a blessing or the reason for him to get up in the morning every day.

His entire demeanor changed, no longer the loveable, approachable Jack he had been. Instead, he became more agitated and confrontational as the days went on. Jack was good right up until he had his first drink of the day, then it was a downward spiral of belligerent and abusive comments for the rest of the evening. What a treat to be around him it was, and Jack chose John as the target of all his verbal lashing. John would walk in with his earbuds, trying to avoid conversation, which would always piss Jack off even more.

"What the fuck! You can't acknowledge anyone when you walk in the house? Who do you think you are, Mr. Fucking Special?!"

By this point in the day, Jack had drunk almost an entire case of beer before his kids got home. This was normally when John would walk into the kitchen and try to find something for him and Mary to eat for dinner. Knowing that Jack was completely unable to cook them a meal, John became the caregiver for himself and Mary—not just with mealtime, but with her homework and everything else in the house. John automatically assumed the responsibility of a parent. It was evident to him his father was useless, although if you asked Jack, he would say it was the other way around.

Jack wasn't an educated man, but, when he spoke, his words were like daggers to a young man's heart. He always had a way of reminding John how much pain he was in, and who he believed was the source of all his suffering.

"Sometimes, son, I think you were the cause of your mother's death and not cancer. You put her through so much stress, pain, and suffering that you caused her to die," Jack would say.

John would stand there stunned like a deer in the headlights, which only caused Jack to add things like, "Oh, don't act like a hurt schoolgirl!"

John would run away to his room quietly, sobbing to himself. God forbid Jack would've heard his *weak* son crying. That would be the end of it. In Jack's eyes, his son would never amount to anything in life, so what was the point in believing in him. It was pointless, a waste of time. John had to figure out how much the world and everyone in it didn't care about him, and Jack was going to teach him.

John had a knack for getting into trouble, starting arguments with teachers just to get removed from class. He was constantly late or absent altogether, which infuriated his father, who would receive phone calls from the school every time his son wouldn't show up for class.

He would say, "Man can take everything from you; your house, your car, all your money, but he can't take your education."

To which John would reply, "Yeah, because you're so smart… That's why you went to trade school."

This would be the point when Jack would become enraged and throw a bottle in John's direction, usually aiming for his head, but always missing.

"You worthless piece of shit. How about you shut the fuck up because you know nothing about anything. The only thing you're good for is getting beers from the fridge and wasting space, so why don't you do what you do best and fuck off and get me a beer!"

John would walk away as Jack continued screaming at him.

"You think that school is going to do anything for you? You're a screw-up, don't you know that? Who's going to give you a job? Who's going to trust you to make real decisions? I don't think you could handle the pressure. You'd probably run away, like a baby, crying to your dead Mommy. Well, son, your mother isn't here to wipe away your tears anymore."

John stopped at the base of the steps and turned to his father as he continued to berate him.

"Face it, boy, no one gives a shit about you. Aren't you ever going to learn that? Why can't you be more like your sister? She has more smarts than both of us combined and, unfortunately for you, you got the shit end of the stick on that one. Time to come to terms with that and move on. It's a shame your mother coddled you all your life… Maybe you wouldn't be so mediocre. Your mother didn't want me to tell you this, but you were a mistake…"

Jack finally stopped talking enough for John to start walking up the steps. This time, he wasn't crying. His face was flushed and red, but John was fed up with his father and his diminished expectation of him. If Jack thought that he was never going to amount to anything, well, John was going to prove him right. He was going to be the best degenerate his family had ever seen.

It was the spring of 2013, John was almost 18, and decided that school was worthless. Seeing as though he wasn't going to college, what was the point in even graduating high school? He thought his time would be better doing whatever he wanted, which, for him, was hanging out in the park, smoking cigarettes, and drinking. At night, he would sneak in through his window to avoid dealing with Jack on the couch waiting to verbally assault him when he walked in the door.

This went on for a few weeks. John would wake up each morning, pretending like he was going to school, then head down to the local corner store, and wait for Robert, the homeless man with salt and pepper hair and a wiry, scratchy beard, to wake up. Then, he would bribe him to buy him beers with the few dollars his father left them for lunch money. He would usually complain for a few minutes until John would agree to buy him a beer, too. John became fast friends with Robert, who drank often and who would on occasion offer John drugs, always plunging a needle into his own arm. John felt at home hanging out with him because he never pressured him to be someone he didn't want to be. Robert didn't belittle him for not being smarter than the person next to him and he didn't compare him to someone else. That's what John appreciated the most—he could just be a young man who wanted nothing more than to hang out in in the park, avoid his problems, and live out the rest of his days as such.

John didn't have time to process his mother's death while he was living in his father's house, but as he sat in the park, he would imagine her and wish that she was alive and not his father. He would dream about what they would do on the weekends, if she might take them on trips to the beach or make cookies during the holidays. He thought about if she would still kiss him good night like when he was little. This led John to a meltdown, which eventually turned into an all-night binge, and John sat in the park with Robert and drank beer.

On one particular night, there was a new hospital band on Robert's arm, but John decided not to mention it. This time, when Robert offered him drugs, he accepted it. He had become comfortable with this lifestyle and saw no problem with it. At this point, he would rarely go home other than to grab clothes or steal any food that was in the fridge.

One day, while John was in the kitchen looking through the cabinet, he heard a noise from the other room. It was his sister, who was home from school early. She walked in and stood in the doorway of the kitchen while John was still bent down looking in the cabinets.

"What are you doing here? I thought you ran away," Mary asked.

"Just stopping by to grab a snack, don't be mad. You know I can't stay here anymore," John said, looking up from the cabinet to see his sister.

"Why would you leave me with him? All he does is complain about you nonstop, and about how much of a screw-up you are," Mary said as she stood back and looked at him.

"So, I guess things haven't changed much," John snapped back.

"No, but that doesn't mean that I don't miss you," Mary said.

"But, Sis, that's exactly why I can't be here anymore. I will never achieve anything more than being a fuck up, this coming from a man who comes home from work and nearly drinks himself to death each night and blames it on his children," John yelled.

He was pacing at this point and forgot that this was the same time his father got home from work. The door opened and Jack stumbled through half-drunk and fuming.

"Who the fuck is screaming in my house! I can hear your ass from the driveway!"

"Me!" John said, standing in the kitchen with his sister right next to him.

He stared at his son for a moment, then looked away. Jack's pride wouldn't allow him to feel any pain for him.

"What are you doing here? I thought you ran away from your family," Jack said sarcastically, walking past his kids to get a beer from the fridge.

"No, I just ran away from *you*!" John responded quickly.

"Well, if you ran away, why the fuck you are standing in my kitchen with my food in your hand, genius?" Jack said, already making his way to the couch.

"Just making sure there was something for my sister to eat because I know how much of a shitty father you are. Lord knows she would starve waiting for you to cook a single meal," John yelled again as he began walking into the family room.

Jack stood up. "Listen, kid, we've been doing fine without you, and trust me, it's been a lot quieter, too. So, if you don't mind, would you shut up and get out! Hug your sister and fuck off, but

---

THE DRINKS BETWEEN US

leave the food on the counter!" he screamed as he popped open the beer he grabbed.

John dropped the can of tuna and the pack of saltine crackers that he had found in the bottom of the cabinet on the table, hugged his sister, and walked out the door. Nothing else needed to be said. It was obvious that this wasn't his home anymore. Jack sat there silently staring at the blank TV screen as his son walked out the door.

At that point, Mary was stuck at home, finishing high school while their father continued coming home every night and drinking himself to sleep. Jack would find a spot on the couch and stay there for years.

THE MAIN STREET BAR
South Jersey, NJ | Spring 2018

John stared at his empty bottle for a minute before moving it toward the edge of the counter. Ben was standing in the middle of the bar, staring at the TV with his mouth open.

"Hey, do you mind?" John said.

"Oh, sorry, got caught up in this show for a minute," Ben replied as he grabbed another beer from the fridge.

Ben had been working at the bar for a while. He had become a good judge of character. Yet, there was something about John that he couldn't pinpoint. He did not pity him, but had seen enough men enter the bar in his same disposition that he empathized with him.

He placed the glass down and walked over to the other man across the bar.

"Need a refill, Mike?" Ben asked, motioning to the almost empty bottle.

"Yeah, I guess it's about that time," Mike replied.

Ben stood there while Mike finished his drink and placed it back on the bar. Then, as Ben went to grab a beer, Mike continued probing John.

"So, let me get this straight. While your father was grieving in silence, what were you doing?" he said.

"Doing the same thing he was doing, drinking to avoid the

---

pain," John snapped.

"What did I say!" Ben barked as he slammed the refridgerator door.

"No, it's alright, Ben, the kid and I are just having a conversation," Mike said calmly.

"Right, we're just having a conversation," John added.

"If you must know, after I left the house, I lived in the park for a little while… Until I decided it was time for me to pack my shit up and move elsewhere," John said, with a sense of sarcasm behind his voice.

"Sounds like you're proud of that or something," Mike said.

"I am not proud of anything, just the way my life ended up," John popped back.

Stumped, Mike sat there quietly for a moment, looking at the label on his beer, before saying, "You must have been a shitty kid for your father to kick you out of the house!"

"What the fuck did you say!" John hollered, slamming his beer so hard on the counter that the bottom cracked open.

Ben snapped, knowing he had a mess to clean up.

"I thought I told you I didn't want that shit in here today!"

"I'm so sorry, man. I'll cool down. He's just starting to piss me off," John said.

Ben shot Mike a stern look, almost an *I told you* in his eyes.

The two men seated in the booth behind John had enough. They ended their last game of chess and carefully approached the bar for their check, avoiding John's and Mike's stares.

"My old man didn't kick me out. I walked out of the house on my own," John told Mike as he took a sip of his beer.

"Listen, kid, I didn't mean anything by it. A lot of people

leave home early and make it on their own. Tell me what you did after you stopped living in the park?" Mike said.

John sighed deeply and waited a second before responding.

"I spent some time in a few shelters. They're okay when it's cold, but I could never really fall asleep, always felt like someone was going to steal my shit. So, most nights, I would walk around the city and make friends with all the homeless guys. They always knew the best dumpsters to dive or where to buy the best drugs. So, either way, I was good."

John thought about the nights when he and Robert would shoot up in the bathroom at the corner store. He picked it because it was the closest to the park, until one night when John overdosed in the stall and the night manager found him and called the cops. This was the second time John had overdosed in the bathroom, but the first time he got caught, and he chose to make sure it was his last. John decided he was tired of living on the street. He figured getting clean and having a warm place to sleep was better than leftover food. John found a free rehab clinic he could go to that would allow him to stay for 90 days.

"How long did you do that for?" Mike asked.

"What? Drugs or living on the street?" John answered sarcastically.

"Both."

"Well, I did heroin for as long as I lived in the park, so about five years, give or take," John said, unapologetically and un-ashamed since he had repeated the story countless times in rehab.

"Okay, and how old are you now?"

"23. What, are you writing a book over there about me?" John said, becoming agitated again.

Mike was a mild tempered man, but John was pushing his limits.

"No, just trying to get the timeline right in my head… So, let me get this straight. You're over there acting like your father is the reason for all your problems?" Mike asked, sitting up in his chair.

"Yup!" John said, proudly.

"But you were the one who left the house, decided to become homeless, and do drugs in the park all day?" Mike shouted, looking across the room at John's silhouette.

"Yes! But my father *drove* me to do it with his condescending tone and his badgering every night! I was never going to be good in his eyes!" John shouted back. "And what for? Me to sit there and listen about how great my sister was? Fuck that! I got better shit to do!"

"Alright, settle down now," Ben cut in.

"I just have one more question, and then, I'll leave you alone. I get it, some of us like to drink our pain away, others like to do other stuff. Whatever helps you keep the demons at bay. No judgment—"

"What's your question, man?" he interrupted.

"So, this whole time you were away from home, did you ever stop to think about what his life was like? I mean, his wife had died. Not to mention, his son was acting like a complete ass and not showing him an ounce of respect?"

"What the fuck did you say to me? Once again, you're talking like you know me," John said, fidgeting in his chair.

"I'm just saying, kid, you got a lot of nerve sitting over there complaining about how rough you had it. Sounds like you brought a lot of that shit on yourself. The drugs, the homelessness, weren't all his fault… Maybe you should give your father the benefit of the doubt," Mike said.

Ben, getting tired of repeating himself, grabbed an empty

shot glass and grabbed John another beer to try and distract him from the conversation.

"Honestly, who the fuck is this guy, thinking he is my therapist or something?" John murmured as Ben brought him the beer.

"Listen, man, how about we lay off the 'father' talk for a while, huh? I'm getting a little tired of the Freud routine," John said.

"Fine," Mike said, trying to calm down.

"Fine," John replied, doing the same.

ROWAN UNIVERSITY
South Jersey, NJ | Winter 2015

It had been years since John had seen his sister. Ever since that day in the kitchen, John knew that he would never see his sister again. Knew he could never go back home or be in the same house with his father again.

At night, while he was getting high in the park, he would think about his sister and what she was doing. How she was dealing with that old man and if she felt the same way he did.

He'd ask himself, *Did she miss Mom the same way I did? Did she hurt every day and wish for her to come back or that it was Dad and not her. Why was I the only one who felt like this?*

Mary was a bright young woman, a star in her father's eyes, and the only thing left in his life worth living for. After John left, Jack was a shell of a man. He worked as little as he could and even less when he came home, not even the bare minimum, cleaning the beer bottles that covered the living room table. Mary was left to live in a damaged home, with no one to raise her and in charge of everything. Her relationship with Jack became nonexistent—the opposite of what it had been like when she was a child. He used to take her on fishing trips, helping her hook the bait, and asking her about her dreams. Sometimes, Jack would let Mary choose the flowers he was bringing home for Margaret, but this was all before she got sick. Now, Mary and her father didn't talk anymore, he didn't ask her about her dreams, and he didn't care about what was happening in her life.

Despite her absent father, she accomplished many things. She was vice-president of the student council and received many awards for her academic achievements. After graduation, she went on to college where she excelled even more. Mary decided to major in medicine, and had dreams of opening a clinic one day. She wanted to be able to help the people in her neighborhood get the care they needed. She wanted the chance to touch everyone's lives in some way.

During her time at medical school, Mary began dating a young man named Chris. They met at a study group for their Anatomy and Physiology class, and Mary instantly found him smart, handsome, and funny. Chris knew Mary was serious about becoming a doctor and would spend his nights in the library or at an off-campus coffee shop, studying with her instead of out with his friends. Mary thought it was sweet. On their walk back to their rooms the night Chris officially asked her to be his girlfriend, they talked about what their life would be like after graduation.

"It won't always be like this," Mary said.

"Like what?" he said.

"So busy… All the studying… Eventually, once we have jobs, we can spend more time together without books in our hands," she said.

He chuckled.

"I don't mind. Books or no books, I love hanging out with you, but yeah, it would be nice to go out to dinner for once," he laughed.

She smiled as he opened the door to her dorm room.

"Soon, I promise," she said.

"I know, don't worry," he said.

Chris leaned in, his hands sweaty from the nerves and kissed her. It was their first kiss and something about it let them know they had found the right one for each other.

RISTORANTE LA BUCA
South Jersey, NJ | Spring 2017

The night before graduation, Chris made reservations at a fancy restaurant in town. He called Mary and told her it was a "no book night" and that they were going out for dinner. He took a taxi and only had to wait a few minutes before being seated.

"This is a really beautiful place," Mary said when she arrived.

"Yeah, I know. I wanted to do something special as a kind of graduation gift," he said.

"Thank you," she smiled, leaning in to kiss him.

The tables were lined with white linen and topped with black plates. Classical music played softly, and the smell of fresh bread and pasta sauce wafted out from the kitchen. The waiter went over the specials for the day and Chris and Mary ordered their food. While they waited, Chris wondered about tomorrow.

"Do you think your dad will show up?" he said.

"I doubt it. I sent him an invitation, but he never called or RSVP'd," she said, dejectedly.

"I'm really sorry," Chris said, reaching to grab Mary's hand.

"It's okay. I have you, right?" she said as the waiter placed a large bowl for carbonara in front of her.

After graduation, it didn't take long for Chris and Mary to

receive job offers at the local hospital, and they were grateful to be working at the same one. They woke up excited for their first day of residency, a day of new beginnings, but Chris was most excited for something else. This was the day he was going to propose.

Chris fiddled with the box nervously as he waited for Mary by the entrance to the hospital. He knew the hospital had been the place where her mother had died and admired her wanting to make a difference in the lives of others where she couldn't for her. He wanted the hospital to be a new, better memory for Mary, starting with the ring in his pocket.

This is it! The start of our new life together, Chris thought.

Mary's heart pounded as Chris got down on one knee to open the ring box.

Just like in my dreams, Mary thought.

"I promise to be the best husband, to love you always and forever because you deserve the very best of everything, and I want you to have it all. Will you marry me?" Chris asked.

"Of course," she said with tears of excitement running down her face.

Chris slid the ring onto her finger and kissed her passionately.

"How do you feel?" he asked as he noticed Mary was still crying.

"I wish my mother was here so I could tell her how happy I am. That I met someone who truly adores me and would do anything for me. But I hope she's proud of me for wanting to take care of people, for loving people like she did. I hope she knows how much I miss her," she replied.

"Your mother would be very proud of you, Mary. You know she's always going to be with you."

Chris held Mary in his arms, wiped the tears from her eyes,

and kissed her forehead. She smiled at Chris and took his hand as they walked into the hospital.

291 ELDERBERRY LANE
South Jersey, NJ | Winter 2017

A year into their new life, Chris and Mary felt things were finally falling into place. They were moving into a one-bedroom apartment together and moving up in their departments at the hospital. Mary had been through so much in her childhood and, while he didn't know the details, he knew enough to know she deserved all the happiness coming her way and he was determined to make her the happiest she could be. He was so excited to start his new life with her, buy a house, and build a family. He knew he had what it took to be a great father.

They had been on opposite schedules for the last few weeks and Mary had volunteered to work the night shift. Mary was always a night owl and enjoyed visiting with patients and talking with them. She was uncommonly kind, similar to her mother in that way, and had a great love for people. On her way home, she would always stop at the local deli and grab coffee for Chris, who would be getting ready for his shift. Sometimes, if she wasn't in a rush, she would buy a cup for the homeless kid who slept on the side of the store. She would think of her brother and if he was still on the streets. Mary had been focused on her life for so long that it was hard for her sometimes to slow down and think about her past.

This morning was similar to most mornings. Mary stopped at the deli to grab coffee. On her way in, she noticed the homeless kid sleeping on the air vent outside the store. As she walked in, she wondered when the last time the kid ate, and about her brother. She made her usual orders of coffee and grabbed a breakfast sandwich for the kid. When she bent down to leave the sandwich next to him, he began to roll over.

With a soft voice, Mary said, "I bought you this sandwich, hope you stay warm."

The kid sat up and took a bite and said, "Thank you, and God bless."

Mary smiled and began to walk away carrying Chris's travel mug. She made it a block away from her apartment before the homeless kid caught up with her.

"Hey, excuse me, can you spare a dollar, please? It would help."

As the kid approached her, she could only think of her brother and the struggles he went through, how hard it must have been. The kid looked gaunt, his face sunken in, and his pupils dark like the night. She felt so sorry for him, and she wished she could do more than just give him a dollar. She wished she could ask where his parents were, why he was sleeping outside of a deli instead of in a bed. *Could he be that bad that his parents wouldn't want him anymore?*

Mary put the travel mug down, so she could look in her purse for her wallet. While she was looking down, the kid tried snatching the bag off her shoulder. Mary caught the strap of the bag and a tug of war began. They pulled back and forth for a few seconds—what felt like an eternity—before Mary let go of the bag. She thought to scream for help, but it was too early and no one else was around.

Afraid that Mary would recognize him and turn him in, the kid pulled out a knife from his jacket pocket and thrusted it into

Mary's back. He stabbed her again and again, blood pouring onto the knife and his hand. Mary, stung by the pain, fell to the ground gasping for air. Panicking, the kid clutched the bag and ran away.

Chris was still at home getting ready when he looked at the clock and noticed Mary hadn't walked through the front door with his travel mug and radiating smile.

She must have gotten caught up talking to one of her patients, he chuckled to himself.

Not wanting to be late for his morning rounds, he left the house and started down the driveway, finding a body laying on the sidewalk a block away. Immediately, Chris jumped out of his car and grabbed his medicine bag from the back seat. It took a second before he realized it was Mary. Checking for a pulse, Chris knew that his fiancée was dead. Trembling, he broke out into tears and stumbled to the car to call the police.

Chris stood there in shock as the police taped off the scene and pulled a sheet over Mary. He stammered as he explained how this was the normal trip she took to get home from work, how kind she was, and how she always helped out the homeless, always buying them coffee because they made her think of her brother. The police explained to Chris that it was most likely a robbery gone wrong and that they would do everything they could to catch the person who did this.

Chris knew very little about Mary's family, only that her father was still alive and that she hadn't seen her brother in years. She rarely talked about them and Chris knew not to push the issue. He knew that her mother had passed away when she was younger and that her father had lived in the same house she grew up in. Her childhood home was a few towns over from where they lived. He remembered the time they stopped by to drop off a few boxes when they first moved back from college. How cold and uninviting the house seemed.

That afternoon, once the police were done interviewing him, he went home to take a shower and thought to drive over to Jack's house to tell him what had happened in person. Standing in the doorway of their apartment with tears in his eyes, Chris wondered how he would explain this to Jack. He barely knew the man, and he had to tell him the awful news of his only daughter.

Chris got dressed and left for Jack's house. He knocked a few times, but there was no answer. Not wanting to leave without giving Jack the news, he knocked once more but harder.

"Hello! Jack! It's Chris, Mary's fiance. Can you open up? We need to talk."

Jack rose from his nap and made his way to the front door to let Chris in. Sitting down on the couch, Chris began to stutter as he explained what happened to Mary. He told him about how he had proposed to her, that they planned to be together and start a family. Jack, still nursing a hangover by taking swigs from an old beer, was trying to process that his daughter was dead. With a sad and confused look on his face, he thought about how tiny she was the first time he held her in his arms. How she reminded him of Margaret and how they both had kind hearts. He thought about how she had accomplished so much, built a life for herself, and fallen in love.

The two men sat in silence for a few minutes before Chris stood up to leave. As they walked to the door, he conveyed his deepest sympathy and told him that he would love to honor her by paying for the funeral process and would let him know when he was making arrangements. Jack accepted the offer of help and told Chris to do what he thought was best for her. Walking back to the car, Chris thought about how he would reach out to her brother.

That night, Chris laid in bed and started looking at old pic-

---

tures of them on Mary's computer. He knew she was looking for her brother on social media, but wasn't sure if she found him. He pulled up the browser and searched for her brother's social media page, but it was already in the search history. She had found him. He hesitated before typing the message out. He wanted to start by explaining who he was and how he was engaged to his sister, then go into what happened to her, how the cops are still looking for her killer, and finish by explaining that he was taking care of her funeral arrangements. Chris put his information at the bottom and the address to his apartment. He knew this was the worst way to find out this kind of news, but he had no other choice and no way to reach John.

It took a day and a half for Chris to receive a call from John, who was out on a job and hadn't checked his phone. He thanked Chris for reaching out and asked if they could meet once he got into town. Chris told John that he would be heading up to speak with the director of the funeral home the following Monday. John offered to join him and Chris agreed. Early the next morning, John woke up, packed his clothes and tools, and jumped on a bus to go home.

By that afternoon, John was back in town, stressed and thinking about his past.

It's all my fault. I never should have left her in that house with him... Fuck that, it's his fault for not taking care of her all those years... Lazy piece of shit!

John became more enraged as he walked the two blocks past the hospital where his mother died. He stopped at the corner in front of a big wooden door, opened it, sat down on a stool at the end of the bar, and asked the bartender for a beer. That was the exact moment when a stranger started asking him questions about his life.

THE DRINKS BETWEEN US

THE MAIN STREET BAR
South Jersey, NJ | Spring 2018

"What brought you back to town, kid? Work?" Mike said.

John paused for a second, then replied, "None of your business!"

His head started to pound as he remembered his baby sister, the one he was supposed to protect, and the reality that she was gone.

"Sorry, kid, I'll quit bothering you, just trying to make conversation."

John sighed deeply as he took a sip of his beer.

"I'm here to take care of my sister, Mary" John's voice cracked a little when he said her name.

John sat there for a few minutes, staring off into space, thinking. He thought about his sister and the last time he had seen her. Leaving the house that day, he thought about if that would be the last time he would see her, knowing that she would be stuck in the house with their miserable father. He felt so bad, but he knew he couldn't stay, that it would be better for her in the long run with him not being there. John sat there, pushed his beer forward, and took a deep sigh.

With a shallow voice, he said, "I'm here to bury my little sister… to help with the funeral arrangements."

Mike cleared his throat, sure at this point that he knew who was sitting at the other end of the bar. It was Jack's son. But he wasn't about to let him know he knew his father.

"I'm sorry to hear that," was all he managed to say.

John, who was just staring at the beer, scoffed at himself.

"Yeah… You have no idea."

Mike sat there wondering if he should give the kid a minute. He could see John was shaken up. He wasn't acting like the rude and cocky kid from before. He could see defeat in his slouching shoulders. Mike got up from his seat, slid his beer to the edge of the bar, and gestured at Ben for another beer. He walked across the bar and avoided bumping into John on the narrow strip of space to the bathroom.

"Hey, who the fuck is this guy sitting here asking me all these questions about me and my shit?"

"He's been coming for a while now. He sits in the same spot and drinks the same drinks. He started coming here a while back when his wife died."

155 WELLINGTON AVE
South Jersey, NJ | Autumn 2005

One evening, after Jack came home from work, still numb from losing Margaret, a card fell out of his wallet when he took it out of his pocket and placed it on the dresser. He picked it up off the floor and looked at it for a moment. It was the grief counseling card the nurse had given him a few weeks before, right after Margaret's death. Jack finished getting changed and picked up the card to call the director.

Maybe this will help stop the pain... he thought.

Speaking to the director, there was an open session that night. It had been a while since Jack had walked through the front doors of the hospital where his wife had died, but he still knew his way around the hospital despite wanting to forget all the changes it had brought to his life. He made his way down to the rec room where he saw the grief counseling flyer. Something caught in his throat.

Maybe this is a dumb idea... I don't think this is going to work, he thought.

The staff had removed all the tables in the room and there was a circle of chairs in the middle of the floor. One table was left on the side for coffee and store-bought cookies. There was a low murmur in the room as people settled down into their seats.

The director started off by introducing himself and asking

everyone to go around the room and say their name. Then, he asked if there were volunteers who wanted to share their story with the group. Person after person shared heartbreaking stories about losing a loved one as Jack tried to avoid eye contact and speaking altogether. Seated directly across from him was a rough-and-tough kind of guy, someone who seemed just as out of place as Jack felt He had introduced himself as Mike and began to share his story, struggling to get the words out at the toughest points. Jack started to notice the similarities between the two of them. He sat there intently listening until the director asked if anyone else wanted to share. He sat back and looked at his shoes, hoping the director wouldn't notice him. After a few moments of awkward silence, the director told everyone they were done for the evening. As the last of the group members converged on the coffee table, Mike and Jack stood there spinning the coffee stirrers in the cups.

"Jack."

"Mike."

The men greeted each other, unsure what to say next.

"I usually go for something stronger than this. I know a bar a few blocks away. Want to grab a drink?" Jack asked, setting his black coffee cup down on the table.

"Sure, why not?" Mike said, ditching his own coffee.

The two of them walked the two blocks to The Main Street Bar, which had become a watering hole for sad men and sat down at the counter to order a drink. They didn't talk much. Jack sat deep in thought, replaying his last days with Margaret while Mike looked around, distracted by the aesthetic of the dim-lit bar he'd never been to, the news barely audible over the blaring jukebox. It wasn't until the beers arrived that the mood was lifted. A sense of peace washed over them though they still sat in silence.

THE MAIN STREET BAR
South Jersey, NJ | Spring 2018

Mike walked out of the bathroom, eyeing his spot to see if Ben had replenished his beer. Walking back to his seat, he heard John's words and stopped in his tracks.

"Just because his wife died doesn't mean he can sit here and give me life lessons."

"You insolent child… Do you have any idea what it feels like to watch someone die? To slowly lose the love of your life? To sit by her bedside every goddamn day and be powerless to help her… Do you know how that feels?" screamed Mike ferociously into John's face.

"No, I don't," responded John under his breath, staring at Mike in the eyes for the first time.

"How about we all relax for a little? Here, shut up and drink this. It's too early to be this drunk," Ben said, pushing a tall glass of water in front of John.

"I'm sorry, Ben. That was uncalled for," Mike apologized, feeling ashamed for his outburst.

"All good, Mike. How about we change the subject, huh?" Ben asked, pointing with his head for Mike to return to his seat.

Mike walked slowly to his seat, thinking about Ben's words. Decidingly, he chose to ignore them. Mike was tired of listening to John complaining about his father. John had no idea what Jack had gone through, but Mike was going to make him understand how it felt.

You may have lost the same person, but it is not the same, Mike thought.

"Tell me a little about your sister," he said, taking a swig of the beer Ben had left out for him.

"Look, man, I'm not trying to be rude, but how about you leave me alone, okay?"

"Sorry, kid. I don't mean to keep poking the bear. I just know a little bit about loss. Thought it might help to think about something nice for a change," he retorted.

"Is that what the therapist keeps telling you to do? How's that working for you?" John replied sarcastically, thinking the other man must be bold to think he can come in here and psychoanalyze him.

I just met this guy today. He knows nothing about me. He hasn't spent more than a few hours with me and now he thinks he has me all figured out. I hate when people assume that they know someone just from a little bit of conversation, John thought.

He mumbled to himself under his breath before taking another sip of his water while Mike sat back for a second.

"Listen, kid, I don't presume to know everything, but I do know that the world is not set in stone and that your life can change within an instant… I woke up one day, a husband, and went to bed, a widower. You think I wanted that to happen to me? You think I wanted to lose my best friend? You think you have control over your destiny, but you don't… I thought I had it all figured out. I had a beautiful wife, happy kids, and a decent job. I wasn't a rich man, but I had enough. Then, one day, the doctors told us she had cancer. I spent every day in that hospital room, machines beeping all around me, and then, she was taken away from me. I don't pretend to know your life, but I do know about loss. I made a life for myself, something you probably know nothing about," Mike said.

John was stunned. He sat there thinking about what he was going to say next. He was fuming inside.

Who the fuck is this guy to sit here and compare his shit life to mine just because he woke up one day and his wife died? That doesn't have anything to do with me.

John cleared his throat before saying, "You listen here, old man, I don't know you and I'm tired of this conversation! No one wants to hear your sad story!"

"It sounds like God dealt you a shitty hand," Mike retaliated.

"Why don't you give up?" John replied, annoyed.

"Clearly, you're not listening to me," Mike laughed, "My point is that sometimes shit happens to you and there are so many more things you can do besides sit there and bitch and moan for the rest of your life."

"Fuck you, man. You don't know what I've gone through living in that house, how he made me feel small and worthless every day. There were days when I wouldn't want to get out of bed. I didn't see the point in going to school, in coming home to see his drunk ass on the couch, bitching at me once I hit the doorway. I didn't want to come home to a house where I secretly envied my sister for being the one who got all the praise, all the love, all the attention. I feel like a complete asshole for feeling that way. Now that she's gone, I'm trying to hold onto what little life I have left without completely falling apart. Get it? It's absolutely difficult sometimes and there are times when I think the universe is totally against me. I told you that I had a fucked up childhood and a terrible father. I'll admit maybe some of that had to do with my poor choices, and yes, you're right, I did it to myself. But don't assume that I don't know shit and that I haven't been through anything because I have!"

Ben had had enough of their back and forth.

"Alright, you guys! That's enough, both of you are done," Ben said. Turning to John, he added, "It's time for you to leave. I'm calling you a cab. What hotel are you staying at, kid?"

Ben walked over to John who was standing at the bar wobbling back and forth.

"Let's go, I'm done with you," Ben said.

Sternly, he added, "Drink!" and handed John the water. He then stared at him and signaled him to drink more.

A few minutes passed before the cab pulled up out front and honked the horn twice, signaling its arrival.

Ben walked with John to the front door and said, "Okay, that's your ride, time to go!"

John walked to the big wooden door, staring at the floor. The long day of drinking hit John very hard and his surroundings started to spin, becoming disoriented. As he passed by the other man, he started to mumble something indiscernible. Ben began to push him out the door, fearing that another fight would ensue. Mike, who had jumped out of his seat, thinking John might attack him, shook his head as he finished his beer.

Ben walked back into the bar and came around to Mike.

"Sorry about that, boss. How about another drink on me?"

"Sure. Why not?"

Mike sat back down for a second, thinking about what happened—the conversation he had with this kid, who made him think about his life and his kids—and wondered if he was that man, if he could be the shitty dad that this kid was talking about.

"On second thought, I think it's time for me to head out,"

he said.

He paid his tab, stood up and pulled his jacket off the back of the chair.

"Sorry again about that kid. He doesn't know what the fuck he's talking about," Ben said as he picked up the check from the counter.

"Don't sweat it."

Ben, frustrated and confused, responded with "Yeah, you're right."

Mike crossed the bar, opened the door, and the light from outside gently cascaded into the bar as he walked out, the same way it had when he walked in hours earlier.

THE DRINKS BETWEEN US

155 WELLINGTON AVE
South Jersey, NJ | Spring 2018

Jack was sitting on the couch in the living room, staring into the doorway of the kitchen, thinking about the last conversation he had with his son. He remembered the day they argued in the kitchen. John had been so defiant and rebellious, thinking that he knew everything, thinking that he was right about everything.

Jack thought to himself, *What did I do wrong? I did the same thing my father did... Tough love makes you a better man. There are no shortcuts in life.*

He walked into the kitchen, grabbed a beer from the refrigerator, and walked into the living room to sit back on the couch. He sat there in the dark room still thinking about the last time he saw John, replaying the conversation with Chris. Jack got up from the couch and walked upstairs to his daughter's bedroom. He slowly opened the door and turned on the light. He looked around at the room that had been untouched since she went off to college. On the bed sat two boxes, the ones Mary and Chris dropped off when they first moved back to the area. He stopped for a second, took a deep breath, then opened the first box. He looked down to find textbooks and school supplies. Jack opened the second box and found a bunch of pictures of Mary and her friends, a jewelry case her mother gave her before she passed, and a diary stuffed at the bottom of the box.

Jack pulled the diary out of the box and put the lid back on top. He started thumbing through the book as he began walking back downstairs to the kitchen to grab another beer. He put his thumb in between the pages to keep his place as he opened the door to the refrigerator.

As Jack walked to the living room to sit down, he started reading the entry:

"It's been six months since John left and I miss him so much. It's not the same here. Dad is constantly wasted and falling asleep on the couch. There's never any food in the house, and I always end up staying at one of my friend's houses for dinner, not that he would ever notice. John was right. I should have just left when I had the chance. Now, I'm stuck here..."

Jack took a long sip of his beer before putting it down on the coffee table.

Why do my children hate me so much? Was I that terrible of a father?

Jack picked up the diary and finished reading the end of the entry.

"I love my dad and I know he's sad Mom is gone, and I'm sad, too. I think about her every day, and at night, I lay in my bed wishing she were still here to tuck me in and kiss me on the forehead. But she's gone now, and everything has changed, and now I feel like I've gone from one happy family to no family at all. I love Dad, but we still have to get on with our lives and it's not fair to abandon your family while you're still alive..."

Jack sat there thinking about his childhood, about how distant and cold his father was, and how he didn't have a single good memory. He was a terrible father. He was there, but he wasn't there. Jack had wasted precious time with his son and daughter, the time he could have spent watching them grow up.

And what would become of John? he thought. *Would he grow up, mean and angry, like his drunk father, or was there time to change. Time for both of us to change.*

John had been furious that day when he walked out of the house and Jack could hear the anger and sadness in his voice. He could hear it as he sat in the living room, thinking about his own father and how much like him he'd become. So angry and hurtful. Jack refused to end up like him and repeat the patterns.

Had too much time passed? Jack wondered, *Would he even want to talk to me?*

Jack's mind raced as he thought about what had happened to his family, how everything fell apart. He sat on the couch in silence, late into the evening, before walking upstairs to his bedroom. A room he had not slept in in years. Jack spent his nights on the couch because he couldn't sleep in his bed anymore, the bed he and Margaret shared. At night, when the kids were asleep, he would sit in the living room getting drunk, looking at old photo albums she made. But, that night, he slept in the bed that was always perfectly made, and before he got in bed, he laid out his favorite suit on the armchair that sat in the corner of the room, preparing for his daughter's funeral that would occur in the coming days.

BALDWIN FAMILY FUNERAL HOME
South Jersey, NJ | Spring 2018

The next morning, John woke up in his hotel room with a pounding headache. He stumbled to the table, looking for his phone, trying to piece together the events of the day before. He remembered getting into town and stopping at the bar for a few beers. He remembered talking with a man, and that they argued about family. John wiped his eyes as he looked at his phone. One missed call from Chris. John ran to the bathroom to splash water on his face, stumbling around as he tried to put on his best shirt and tie. He called a cab and directed it to the funeral home.

The cab pulled up and John got out, walking down to the front. He texted Chris that he was out front and made his way through the lobby.

Chris came out of the office and said, "Hey, you must be John. Sorry we have to meet like this."

John greeted Chris, shaking his hand and following him back into the office.

The funeral home wasn't far from Jack's house, and after a cup of coffee, he made his way to the door, grabbing Mary's diary off the coffee table before he left. As he pulled into the parking lot, Jack was anxious and clouded with emotions. He walked toward the front door and out walked a tall skinny kid that he recognized immediately. John stood in front of the funeral home with a cigarette in his hand.

When John saw him, he scoffed.

They stood there silently, staring at each other for a minute before Jack cleared his throat and said, "Now, before you say anything, I want to say sorry for being an awful father. I know now that I abandoned you kids and I'm sorry for that..."

John was taken back and decided to let his father finish.

"I know I wasn't much of a father to you when you were younger, but if you give me a chance, I would like to make up for that."

John, wanting to remove himself from this situation, lit his cigarette, took a drag, and exhaled.

"Listen," he said, "I had a rough night and it's not going to get any better today. But I had a conversation with a man last night and he got me thinking... It's been a while between you and me, and I think it's time to bury the hatchet, for Mary's sake."

Jack stood there for a second, shocked and happy.

Clearing his throat again, he said, "Great, I'm happy to hear you say that."

"What should we do first?" Jack added with a half-smile.

"Well, I'm not going home and having a catch with you in the front yard, that's for sure!" John said jokingly.

Jack chuckled and took a step back before saying, "How about we start with food first. Dinner tonight?"

John stood there, biting his lip as he flicked his cigarette. "Fine."

"Good, I'll meet you at Fieni's."

Jack handed the diary to John and John stared at it for a long time.

"I found that in your sister's things last night... You should read it when you get a chance. She did miss you a lot and I'm sure she would have loved to see you again."

John sighed and they both stood in silence.

A few minutes passed until Chris walked out the front door. He greeted Jack and knew it would have made Mary happy to see her brother and father talking to each other.

"They're ready for us."

EPILOGUE

FIENI'S RISTORANTE
South Jersey, NJ | Spring 2018

Jack arrived at the restaurant a few minutes early. He'd forgot to make a reservation and hoped there was still a table open. He walked in to the small Italian place they'd been to so many times before Margaret's death. It was also Mary's favorite place to eat as she loved their homemade pasta. Jack stood in front of the host stand, waiting for him to get off the phone.

Why did I say this place? We're never going to get a table, he thought.

"How can I help you?" said the hostess as she put down the phone.

"A table for two, if you still have one," Jack said.

"You're in luck, a table just opened up. They're cleaning it now. How about a drink at the bar while you wait?"

"Sure, why not," Jack replied as he followed her to the bar.

John walked the few blocks from his hotel to the restaurant. It was a perfect spring night, with just a little breeze, and it had been years since John walked through his old neighborhood. He reached the front door and paused for a moment. He lit a cigarette to ease the nerves and started pacing back and forth.

Why did I come here? It's not like anything is going to change. This is pointless. It's not like he's going to take back the things he said. I know he's not, John thought.

Inside the reseturant, Jack had finished his drink as the hostess tapped him on the shoulder and told him his table was ready. As he walked to the table, he looked at his watch nervously.

This was stupid, he's not coming, he thought to himself.

"I'll have the waiter come by with some water in a few minutes and some menus. Do you know when the other party is arriving?" the hostess asked.

"Soon," Jack said.

At least I hope he is, he thought.

John put out his cigarette and pulled his phone out of his pocket to look at the time. It was five minutes after seven o'clock and he'd watch a few people come and go through the door.

This is a waste of time, he's not coming... he thought.

As he was about to walk toward the curb to hail a taxi, he thought to himself, *Fuck it, I should at least go in and get a drink.*

John opened the door and walked into the crowded restaurant up to the hostess' podium.

"Looks busy tonight. Is there any room at the bar?" he asked.

"I believe a space just opened up," she said, pointing to the empty chair were Jack was sitting.

John walked over to the chair and was about to pull it out when he heard his name called.

"John!" Jack said.

John turned around to see his father sitting at a table a few feet away. He paused for a moment before walking over to the table.

He reached the table and Jack stood up as John pulled out his chair. The two men hadn't been this close to each other in years.

"Thank you for coming," Jack grinned.

"You're welcome," John said quietly.

The two sat in awkward silence until the waiter returned with water glasses and menus.

"Can I start you off with something to drink?" he asked.

"Yes, I'll do a whiskey and a beer" Jack said.

"Same please," John said.

Moments later, the waiter returned with their drinks. The two men, still not speaking, hoped the drinks would help break the tension.

After a few sips, some of the strain had disappeared.

"How about a toast?" Jack asked, raising his glass.

"Sure, I guess," John said, sarcastically.

"Here's to new beginnings?" Jack asked nervously.

It took John a moment to raise his glass, too. The conversation with the man at the bar seemed to play out in his head as he stared at his aged and apologetic father.

Sometimes, we all deserve another chance, he thought.

John raised his glass and offered his old man an honest smile.

"To new beginnings."

ACKNOWLEDGMENTS

ACKNOWLEDGMENTS

I initially wrote this story for me, but throughout my time writing it, each one of these people contributed to the story in one way or another. For that, I give my thanks.

I would like to thank my publisher, Indie Earth Publishing, and my editor, Flor Ana Mireles. She encouraged me to be a better writer, and throughout the process, has been truly amazing. I couldn't be more happy with this project. Indie Earth Publishing's attention to detail, care for artistic ownership, and love for the art of writing made working on this book feel seamless. I appreciate the time and effort put into making my passion project a reality, and I look forward to our next project together.

I would like to thank and acknowledge my parents. Without them, I would not be here. Thank you for ensuring I had all the opportunities I could to achieve greatness and for pushing me to always be the best version of myself. I hope this makes you proud.

I would like to acknowledge Jerry Kendra. He is the reason this book is possible. He was the one who encouraged me to take my idea and run with it. To just start writing and see where the story would take me. I thank you for seeing the potential in me and not letting me waste my talent.

To my partner, Megan, thank you for your continuous support and love. Without you, I wouldn't have had the courage to follow my dream. You're my inspiration.

To the rest of my family and friends, thank you for your love and support.

Finally, I would like to thank my readers because you're a

major part of why I wanted to publish this book, so that I could have it out in the world for all of you to enjoy.

AN INTERVIEW WITH
VINCENT J. HALL II

AN INTERVIEW WITH
VINCENT J. HALL II

Indie Earth Publishing: *The Drinks Between Us* is your debut book. What inspired you to write this story?

Vincent J. Hall II: I think the human condition is fascinating—how people interact with each other, how certain events shape people's lives, and how they react to those events. I had always wanted to write a story, but I didn't know where to start. The initial idea was for the story to be written as a script for a short film. I liked the idea of two people having a conversation in a dark bar, both seated on opposite ends. I wanted the characters to have a real, genuine, emotional converstaion. To be able to reveal parts of themselves that they wouldn't normally because it's easier to talk to a stranger than to say it to the person you need to. I explained my idea to a friend and he encouraged me to start writing it. Once I started writing, I enjoyed where the story was going and decided that it would be best as a short story.

IEP: This book covers some deep topics on alcoholism, drug abuse, generational trauma, and family dynamics. What interested you in exploring these concepts?

VJHII: Each of these topics are very relevant to me. I've experienced and know others who've experienced similar stories. They might have a friend or family member who struggles with alcoholism or drug abuse. They might be someone who's experienced trauma and knows that trauma runs in their family. Or they may have a difficult home life that has strained the relationships with the people they love.

IEP: Was this a difficult subject matter for you to write about? What was the writing process like?

VJHII: I picked the subject matter because I have experience in it and I knew it could trigger a response in me. It became a healing process for me; a way to get out the emotions I had bottled up for years. I started writing the story in 2018. In the beginning, I worked on it in short bursts because I struggled to figure out the direction I wanted to take the story. I would write a section or a scene, then I wouldn't even look at the story. Then, I'd get inspired by a movie or show and I would make myself write again. After that motivation simmered, I wouldn't write. I took a break from the story completely for a few months, but in March 2020, due to the pandemic, I had the opportunity to work from home and I decided to start writing again. I wanted to finish this project since I was stuck at home every day. My process stayed the same, with me working on it periodically, until I finished it in March 2022.

IEP: *The Drinks Between Us* is set in New Jersey. Is there a particular reason you chose this setting?

VJHII: I chose New Jersey because it is the state I grew up in and I wanted the story to be based in the same state where I spent most of my life.

IEP: Knowing New Jersey's significance to you, are any of the settings in the book actual locations or inspired by actual places?

VJHII: A few are actually real places. It's hard to write a story about an real town/area without putting in some aspects of the town. I wanted to story to have bits of the places I grew up with. For instance, in the epilogue, when Jack and John meet for dinner, Fieni's is a real restaurant, but I changed parts of the interior. I also wanted readers from that area to make a connection with some of the places. Chris and Mary go to Rowan University, which is a real college in South Jersey. There are also places that were completely made up. Like, the funeral home named after James Baldwin, one of my favorite authors, or Mr. Scoops, which I think is still a great name for a ice cream place. The addresses were inspired by old homes I used to live by growing up as well.

IEP: You mention that James Baldwin is one of your favorite authors. What authors do you feel influence your writing, if any? Were there any books you read to help you prepare to write or inspire writing for this one?

VJHII: Since I originally wanted to write this as a script, I took my inspiration from movies. From the start, and especially during the pandemic, I watched a ton of movies. All different types of genres—drama, comedy, rom-com, thrillers, etc. I wanted to watch people exhibiting different emotions so I could learn how to express them more naturally. Sometimes, I learned something. Other times, I just watched a movie. But, I recently read *Beloved* by Toni Morrison and I learned a lot about telling stories by using flashbacks. I drew similarities since I wrote about the current happenings in the bar, but flashed back to different points in Jack, John, and Mary's lives just like Morrison did.

IEP: You've created an interesting and vivid cast in this book. Which one did you have the most fun creating? Which character are you rooting for the most?

VHJII: Jack was probably my most fun character to create. I wanted him to be detestable, but also redeemable. It was interesting trying to make a character that, at the beginning of the story, most people would hate and, by the end, had made you changed your mind. He's also the one I'm rooting for the most. It seems like Jack has lost everything, his entire family, but after a moment of self-reflection, he's able to realize he hasn't lost everything yet. And it's in that moment that I see the hope for a better relationship with John and hope that he can be a better father in the future.

IEP: What do you want the reader to take away from this story?

VJHII: There is always time to rebuild that bridge with that certain person in your life. So much happened between Jack and John that it seems like there's no way they'd speak again, but despite the hurtful things he said and all the things that happened, both Jack and John are making the effort to repair their relationship. My hope is that this story helps people heal and encourages them to mend those broken relationships with their loved ones. Trauma can be generational so we have to do whatever we can to break the cycle or we'll transfer that hate, anger, and sadness to the next generation. Jack's anger, abuse, and inability to share his emotions comes from his father. He's transfered that to John throughout the story and John is starting the cycle all over again in his life. It's only when Jack realizes he has made mistakes that he has the opportunity to break the cycle, and the same goes for John. It's only when he has that conversation at the bar with Mike that he thinks about his actions and wants to try to understand and forgive his father.

IEP: Do you have any advice for aspiring authors and writers?

VJHII: Just start writing and it will come to you. A good friend of mine told me this and I think it truly helped me. I had an idea in my head for so long and it wasn't until he said that that I realized I had wasted time I could have spent writing. Sometimes, the ideas will come pouring out of your fingers faster than you can type them. Other days, you'll have absolutely nothing. But just start writing, even if it's just a sentence, even if you erase the next one. Just start and it will come to you. Then, find a great editor—*hint hint* Flor Ana Mireles.

IEP: A lot of readers have truly enjoyed reading this book. Will we be seeing more works from you?

VJHII: I think so. I'm taking my own advice and starting to write a new story. I really enjoyed writing this story and I hope the next story will be as fulfilling and meaningful to me as it was to write *The Drinks Between Us*.

ABOUT THE AUTHOR

ABOUT THE AUTHOR

Vincent J. Hall II is a New Jersey-based writer who made his literary debut with *The Drinks Between Us.* A founding member of the New Jersey Arts and Culture Administrators of Color (NJACAC), he has most recently collaborated with the New Jersey Theatre Alliance (NJTA) on Creating Change Symposium, a virtual conference to help move New Jersey's cultural community to a more just, antiracist, and equitable community. A History graduate from William Paterson University, Vincent helps lead ArtPride New Jersey Foundation's advocacy and governmental affairs efforts and is the new state captain for Americans for the Arts (AFTA)'s Annual Arts Action Summit. He is also an integral part of advancing ArtPride's equity, diversity, and inclusion initiatives and is the staff liaison for the Independent Advisory Committee.

When he is not helping his community and making a difference, Vincent enjoys attending Phillies games with his partner

---

Megan, going to art museums, and going out to dinner with friends. Vincent wants readers to know to not be afraid of the light within them and to follow their dreams wherever they may take them

He says, "When you're afraid, remember this quote from Marianne Williamson: 'Our deepest fear is not that we are inadequate. Our deepest fear is that we are powerful beyond measure. It is our light, not our darkness that most frightens us.' Remember: Don't be afraid to let your light shine."

YOU CAN LEARN MORE ABOUT
VINCENT J. HALL II
AT WWW.LINKEDIN.COM/IN/VINCENTHALL2

CONNECT WITH VINCENT ON INSTAGRAM:
@VINCEVANGOAH

ABOUT THE PUBLISHER

ABOUT THE PUBLISHER

INDIE EARTH
PUBLISHING

Indie Earth Publishing Inc. is an author-first, independent publishing company based in Miami, FL, dedicated to giving artists and writers the creative freedom they deserve in publishing their poetry, fiction, and short stories. We provide our authors a plethora of services that are meant to make them feel like they are finally releasing the book of their dreams, including professional editing, design, formatting, organization, advanced reader teams, and so much more. With Indie Earth Publishing, you're more than just another author, you're part of the Indie Earth creative family, making a difference in the world, one book at a time.

FOR INQUIRIES, PLEASE VISIT
WWW.INDIEEARTHBOOKS.COM

OR EMAIL:
INDIEEARTHPUBLISHINGHOUSE@GMAIL.COM

INSTAGRAM: @INDIEEARTHBOOKS